I can't believe it
Out of all the millions of people
in hundreds of countries
and thousands of cities
I was able to find
my true heart
my true soul
my true love...
you

— Susan Polis Schutz

To My One True Love

You Will Always Be the Only One for Me

Susan Polis Schutz

Blue Mountain Press™

Boulder, Colorado

Library of Congress Control Number: 2010934714
ISBN: 978-1-59842-579-6

◼and Blue Mountain Press are registered in U.S. Patent and Trademark Office.
Certain trademarks are used under license.

Printed in China.
First Printing: 2010

✪ This book is printed on recycled paper.

This book is printed on paper that has been specially produced to be acid free (neutral pH)
and contains no groundwood or unbleached pulp. It conforms with the requirements of the
American National Standards Institute, Inc., so as to ensure that this book will last and be
enjoyed by future generations.

Blue Mountain Arts, Inc.

P.O. Box 4549, Boulder, Colorado 80306

Contents

You Will Always Be the Only One for Me

I always want to be with you
    more than with anyone else
I always want to talk to you
    before anyone else
I always want to laugh with you
walk with you
read with you
play with you
be quiet with you
be noisy with you
make plans with you
discuss the past and future with you
You will always be the person who makes me
happy, content, excited and peaceful
No matter how much time passes
our love will not only prevail
but it will be stronger than ever

I Love You for So Many Reasons

Before I met you
I spent a lot of time
meeting all kinds of people
I had a lot of fun
and learned a lot
Though each person I met
had great characteristics
something was missing
No one person
had all the qualities that
I had hoped a person could have —
someone whose every action
and thought I could respect
someone who was very intelligent
yet could also be fun-loving
someone who was sensitive, yet virile
exciting and sensuous
someone who knew what they wanted
    out of life
a beautiful person inside and out
I could not find a person like this
until I met you

The Day We Met, I Knew My Life Would Never Be the Same

When we met
I knew that you were extremely special
I knew that I wanted to get to
    know you better
When I fell in love with you
I knew that I wanted to spend all my time
    with you
When you and I became one
I knew that I wanted our relationship
    to last forever
If we had not met
I would still be searching for happiness
and I would always be thinking that
    love was not real
So I want to dearly thank you
for the day we met

In Case You Ever Need to Know...

Once in a while
everyone needs
to know that they
are wanted
that they are important
that they are loved

I just wanted
to tell you
that if you
ever feel this need
I would like
to be the one
to reassure you
that you are wanted
that you are important
and that I love you

I Love Everything About You

I love you
for being so honest
for being so free
for being so trusting
for being so passionate
and for contributing so much
to our relationship

I love you
for all you do for me
for all you express to me
for all you share with me
and for all that you are

I love you
for understanding me
for laughing and crying
with me
for having fun with me
and for being such
an outstanding person

I love you
for being so strong
for being so independent
for being so creative
and for being such a unique person

I love you
for all these things and more
I love you
for everything about you

I love you

*You are the
words of my poems
love of my dreams
passion of my dance
notes of my song
spirit of my soul
emotion of my heart*

*I don't know
how you do it!
You are always
so positive and uplifting
so self-contained and occupied
so in charge and confident*

*You are always
so understanding and caring
so vibrant and consistent*

*And I am always
so in love
with you*

Love Is...

*L*ove is being happy for the other person
    when that person is happy
    being sad for the other person
    when that person is sad
    being together in good times
    and being together in bad times
Love is the source of strength

Love is being honest with yourself at all times
    being honest with the other person
        at all times
    telling, listening, respecting the truth
    and never pretending
Love is the source of reality

Love is an understanding so complete that
you feel as if you are a part of the other person
accepting that person just the way he or she is
and not trying to change each other
to be something else
Love is the source of unity

Love is the freedom to pursue your own desires
while sharing your experiences
with the other person
the growth of one individual alongside of
and together with the growth
of another individual
Love is the source of success...

Love is the excitement of planning
things together
the excitement of doing things together
Love is the source of the future

Love is the fury of the storm
the calm in the rainbow
Love is the source of passion

Love is giving and taking in a daily situation
being patient with each other's
needs and desires
Love is the source of sharing

Love is knowing that the other person
will always be with you
regardless of what happens
missing the other person
when he or she is away
but remaining near in heart at all times
Love is the source of security

Love is the source of life

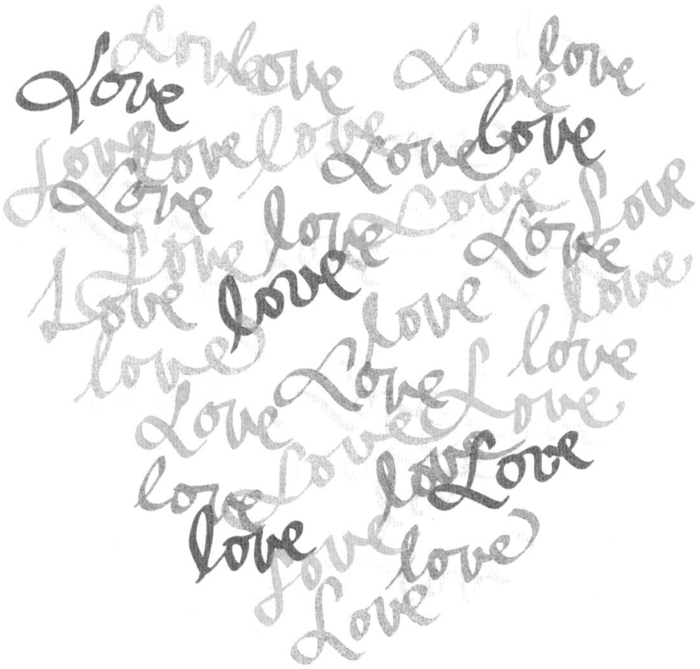

I Always Dreamed How Love Should Be

When I was younger I dreamed
how a relationship should be
a sharing of goals
and lives
a love so strong that
it is always exciting and growing
a blending of two imperfect individuals
into stronger, better people
who laugh more, accomplish more
are happier, more successful
and more at peace

In my dreams
I pictured a person
who was
intelligent, good-looking
sensitive, talented
creative, fun
strong and wise
who would completely
overwhelm me
with love

Since dreams
can be just wishful thinking
I did not really expect
to find one person
who had all these qualities
But then —
I met you
and not only did you
bring back my
belief in dreams
but you are even
more wonderful
than my dreams

I want you to always know
how thankful I am
for our beautiful relationship
and how much I love you

love love love love love love love

Love Is the Most Important Feeling One Can Have

I used to think
that love was only real in the movies
and that I enjoyed being alone

I used to think
that I was too independent
that I didn't need anyone
because I was so strong
But after meeting you
I realized that my attitude
toward love
was merely a cover-up of
my disappointment with relationships
I put on a strong, noncaring front
so no one would know how I felt
But after meeting you
I could no longer pretend
My feelings became transparent
and now I want to tell the world
something I always knew but was
    afraid to admit
that love is the most important
feeling one can have
and I want to thank you for
causing me to be honest
    with myself and others

I Never Want to Be
Without You

Sometimes I wake up
in the middle of the night
shivering from fright
feeling empty
feeling nothing
because I think about
how it would be
if you weren't here
And then I wonder
if you really know
how very much
you mean to me
how incredible
I think you are
how you are
a part of all my emotions
how you are
the deepest meaning in my life
Please always know
that I love you
more than anything else
in the world

Sometimes I worry about you
You don't relax enough
You work so hard
There is so much for you to do
You don't realize how much
*   you are appreciated*
or how much you give
*   of yourself to others*

Other times I am thankful
for the way you are
as I realize it is the
only way you could be

But at all times I want you to know
that I respect you so greatly
and I thank you for
being the best man in the world
in every way

I will support you
in all that you
do
I will help you
in all that you
need
I will share with you
in all that you
experience
I will encourage you
in all that you
try
I will understand you
in all that is in your
heart
I will love you
in all that you
are

On This Day
and Every Day...

You are
my truth
my balance
my honesty
my touch
my sensitivity
my ecstasy
my beauty
my reality
my soul
my life
my sky
my stars
my wind
my sun
my waves
my mountain
my rainbow
my rose
my volcano
You are
my world
my love

I Am So Lucky
to Have Met You

I look at your face
It is so strong
I look at your eyes
They are so soft
I hear you speak
Your words are so wise
I watch your actions
You are such an individualist
I talk to you
You understand the meaning behind
    whatever I say
You are everything
that is beautiful
I am so lucky
to have met you
and I want to
tell you
over and over again that
I have fallen in love with you
and the more
I learn about you
the more
I love you

*M*any people
go from one thing
to another
searching for happiness
But with each new venture
they find themselves
more confused
and less happy
until they discover
that what they are
searching for
is inside themselves
and what will make them happy
is sharing their real selves
with the one they love

When You're Not Here, I Can't Stop Thinking About You

I didn't want to face
being apart from you
so I did everything
to avoid thinking about it
But today I listened to music
    and couldn't run away
I couldn't stop thinking about you
about us
about our deep love
I have gentle tears
because I'm scared
because I'm emotional
because I'm fragile
because I love you
because I miss you

As the notes hit a crescendo
my body shivers
The notes become softer
and a wave of beauty rises
A violin sings a vibrato
reminiscent of your voice
So passionately I feel the music
More passionately I feel
you
But you are there
and I am here
I'm lost
until you are back
My love for you doesn't
travel
It sits within me
consuming every
note of my life

*You went away but
inside my heart
you are with me
I wish you were here
I miss you so much*

I Am Always Thinking of You

It is very rare
to fall in love
with someone like you
who is
so sensitive, yet strong
so caring and understanding
so stable, yet spontaneous
so kind and considerate
so creative, yet practical
I feel like
the luckiest person in the world
because of you
and though
my mind may be occupied
with all the events of the day
you are always at the forefront
of my thoughts
I am always thinking about
how wonderful you are
I am always thinking about
how much I appreciate you
how much I should thank you
and how much
I love you

Even Though We Are Not Together Right Now...

*In the morning
when the sun
is just starting to light the day
I am awakened
and my first thoughts are of you
I miss you*

*In the afternoon
when the sky
is shining brightly
I complete my usual routine
and my thoughts are of you
I see you in my daydreams*

*At night
when the moon
is silhouetted against the quiet stars
I fall asleep
and my last thoughts are of you
Even though we are not together right now
you are a very important part
     of my days and nights*

*W*hat do I miss most?
Your soft skin
your piercing blue eyes
your touch
your words
your sitting at the computer
our walks
our activities
What do I miss most?
Your
everywhere
all-encompassing
loving
quiet
supporting
breathtaking
presence

When you are gone...
The flower has no petals
The tree, no leaves
The bird, no songs

When you are gone
The piano has no notes
The balloon, no air
The sky, no sun
The heart, no beats

Life stops
when you are not with me

When we are together
the whole world seems so far away
and the whole world becomes
you and me
fresh air and flowers
blue sky and birds singing
and a continuous
rainbow of
love

Opening Up to Love

Sometimes it takes
adverse conditions
for people to
reach out to each other
Sometimes it takes
bad luck
for people to
understand their goals better
Sometimes it takes
a storm
for people to
appreciate the calm
Sometimes it takes
being hurt
for people to
be more sensitive to feelings
Sometimes it takes
doubt
for people
to trust one another

Sometimes it takes
seclusion
for people to
find out who they really are
Sometimes it takes
disillusionment
for people to
become informed
Sometimes it takes
feeling nothing
for people
to feel everything
Sometimes it takes
our emotions and feelings
to be completely penetrated
for people to
open up to love
I have gone through
all of these changes
and I now know that
I am more than ready
to love you

I Love You,
Even Though Things
Are Not Always Perfect
Between Us

No one is perfect
therefore no
relationship can be perfect
Often by seeing
the dry brown petals
in a rose
you appreciate more
the vivid red petals
that are so beautiful
At the core of our relationship
there is a very deep respect and love
for one another
so as we continue
to grow and change as individuals
our relationship will continue
to grow stronger
and become more beautiful
I love and appreciate you
so much

I Want Our Relationship to Last

I thought I would never
find the right person
to love
until I met you
And since I have
always thought that
love is the most
important part of my life
I want our love
to last and
to be as beautiful
as it is now
I want our love
to be the backbone
of our lives forever

Our love came naturally
but I know that
we must both work
at making it last
so I will try my hardest
at all times
to be fair and honest with you

I will always
strive for my own goals
and help you achieve yours
I will always
try to understand you
I will always
let you know what I am thinking
I will always
try to support you
I will always
try to successfully blend
our lives together
with enough freedom
to grow as individuals
I will always
consider each day
with you special
Regardless of
what events
occur in our lives
I will always
make sure that our
relationship flourishes
as I will always
love and respect you

Sometimes My Feelings May Be Hurt and It May Seem like I Don't Love You...

Sometimes it may not seem
that I love you
Sometimes it may not seem
that I even like you
It is at these times
that you really need to
understand me more than ever
because it is at these times
that I love you more than ever
but my feelings have been hurt
Even though I try not to
I know that I am acting cold
    and indifferent
It is at these times that I
find it so hard
    to express my feelings

Often what you have done to
hurt my feelings is so small
but when you love someone
like I love you
small things become big things
and the first thing I think about
is that you do not love me
Please be patient with me
I am trying to be more honest
with my feelings
and I am trying not to be so sensitive
but in the meantime
I think you should be very confident that
at all times
in every way possible
I love you

I Am Sorry

After a long day's work
or when I am very tired
every little thing
bothers me
and I will say or do things
which I do not mean
Please realize that my words
are not intended to hurt you
or to be mean
Please realize that
I am only expressing
the frustrations of my day
and since you are with me
at these times
you are the receiver
of my words
I am sorry
I never mean
to hurt your feelings

I dislike so much
the times when
I am angry at you
or when you are
angry at me
We need to
talk about our feelings more
and not harbor resentment
We need to
immediately tell each other
why we feel hurt or mad
so we can make amends
Our days are too short
to waste any time on
not being completely happy
with each other

You Were Made for Me

I often wonder what
made us fall in love with each other
We are so different from each other
Our strengths and weaknesses
are so different
Our ways of approaching things
are so different
Our personalities are so different
Yet our love
continues to grow and grow

Perhaps the differences
we have add to the
excitement of our relationship
and I know that both of us
as a team are stronger
than either of us alone
We are basically different from each other
but we have so many
feelings and emotions in common
And it really doesn't matter
why we fell in love
All that matters to me
is that we continue
to respect and love each other

*Today
I looked at you
standing there under the huge blue sky
and noticed your features —
so strong
I saw your eyes —
so sensitive
I want to be with you
in the wind
in the sun
in the rain
Together always*

I am in love with you
with your strength and your warmth
always thinking
of all the good in life
I am in love with you
with your kindness and truth
always looking
for all the joys in life
I am so proud
when you look at me
so softly
and the world can see
our feelings

There's no one like you
You are
caring
sensitive
understanding
compassionate
smart and
fun

I appreciate your outstanding
uniqueness
There's no one like you
and no one I'd rather be
in love with

You Are My
Soul Mate, My Lover,
My Friend

With you
I can be myself
and I do not have to
pretend to be
anything that I am not
With you
I can say and think everything I want to
and I know that I will be understood

With you
I can be totally free
in body and mind
and I can share my
deepest feelings and emotions
With you
I am filled with a love
that gives me strength and happiness
And I want to thank you for this
and make sure you know that
I love you

You Make Everything in My Life More Meaningful

Whatever I say
means more when
you listen
Whatever I think
means more when
you understand
Whatever I do
means more when
you are there
Whatever happens to me
means more if
I can share it with you
Thank you for
adding so much
to my life

You are so fair
so sensitive
There are no roles
to play with you
You are so different
from everyone else
You are free of pretension
and games
so honest
so good

By loving you
I am learning to be
a better person

Walk *with me in love*
Talk to me about what you cannot say
to others
Laugh with me when you feel silly
Cry with me when you are most upset
Plan with me all your dreams
Share with me all the beautiful things
in life
Fight with me against all the ugly things
in life
Create with me dreams to follow
Have fun with me in whatever we do
Work with me toward common goals
Dance with me to the rhythm of our love
Walk with me throughout life
Let us hug each other
at every step in our journey
forever
in love

Together, We Are Strong

I am so happy with you
I can discuss all my thoughts or
I don't have to say anything
You always understand

I am so relaxed with you
I don't need to pretend
I don't need to look good
You accept me for what I am

I am so strong with you
I depend on you for love
but I live my own life
You give me extra confidence
to succeed

Your heart is my heart
Your truth is my truth
Your feeling is my feeling

But the real strength of
*   our love*
is that we share rather than
control each other's life

Forever forever Forever forever
forever Forever forever Forever
forever Forever forever forever
Forever forever Forever forever
forever Forever Forever forever
Forever forever
forever

I Want to
Love You Forever

I want to be able to
    speak the truth
    be a success in my work
    dress the way I want
yet share my days with you

I want to be able to
    enjoy the activities I like
    adhere to my own values
    act the way I feel
yet share my nights with you

I want to be able to
    be myself and
I want you to be able to
    be yourself
yet share our lives with each other

I want to love you forever

I do not
want to change you
You know what
is best for you
much better than I

I do not
want you to change me
I want you to
accept me and respect me
the way I am

In this way
we can build
a strong relationship
based on reality
rather than a dream

When I see you happy
I, too, am happy
When I see you sad
I, too, am sad
When I see you not feeling well
I, too, do not feel well
When I see you full of energy
I, too, am full of energy
It always amazes me that
though we are two different people
independent in both thought and action
I feel and act the way you do
I guess your moods and feelings
affect me so greatly because
I love you
and I feel so much
a part of you

Thank You for Sharing Your Heart and Your Life with Me

Whenever I make an important decision
I discuss it with you
Whenever I have a difficult day
I know I can forget about it
    by spending time with you
Whenever I have doubts about
    what I am doing
I can always depend on encouragement
    from you
Whenever something special happens to me
your happy reaction makes it
    that much better
Whenever I have new dreams
I can depend on support from you
Whenever I find myself choosing
    the wrong things
a hug from you sets me right again
The most important
thing in my life
is your love
and I am so fortunate to have you
I thank you for sharing your life with me

As Time Goes By, My Love for You Grows Stronger

As time goes by
we know each other better
we share more things together
we have reached or not reached
    so many goals together
we have so many emotions and
    experiences together
As time goes by
the bonds holding us together
the foundation of our relationship
and my feelings of oneness with you
get stronger and stronger
Most of all, my feeling of love
    for you
gets stronger and stronger
as time goes by

Some people believe
that with time
relationships become
less interesting
less exciting and
less fun
But our relationship
with time
has been more interesting
more exciting and
more fun
Some people believe
that with time
the best aspects of
a relationship end
But with time
our relationship
has gotten better and better
and our love has gotten
stronger and stronger
Our relationship is the
most important
part of my life and
I will always strive
to keep it this way

Each Year on Our Anniversary, I Am Reminded of the Promises We Made

On our anniversary
I think back to
when we first met
when we first dated
when we first loved each other
when we first had a disagreement
when we first made up
And I realize that
every day is an anniversary for us
of something we felt together
of something we touched together
of something we shared together
of something we did together

But this day is the most important
milestone of all
It is the anniversary
of the day we
fell in love with each other
Especially today
I want to let you know that
I love being in love with you

All we've been through together
all the changes in our lives and the world
the beautiful easy moments
the sad and difficult times
yet the one continuum in our lives
that has never changed
no matter what was happening
has been our relationship —
our deep love
our respect
our passion
our understanding
our caring
for each other
and this has been the stability
and soul of my life

You are
my fantasy
my dream
my hero
my passion
my best friend
There are no words
strong enough
to describe my overwhelming feelings
    of love for you
We are two people as one
in an emotional, joyous tear

Love Is the Most Beautiful Feeling

When hen you have a person who loves you
unconditionally, passionately
and without judgment
When you have someone who treats you
with respect, understanding
and support
there is nothing more
fulfilling, uplifting
and beautiful

Love is the momentous thrust that
can cause you to reach your goals
It is the one force
that will give life meaning
when nothing else makes sense
It is the thread of peace and security
in a world at odds
It can make you feel like
the most important person on earth
in a world of billions of people
It is the emotion that wakes
your senses to see the beauty
of the sun setting
the flowers blooming
the snow melting
It is the feeling behind
all tears and laughter
It is the most beautiful
feeling of all

When Our Eyes Meet

Sometimes I am
in a room full of people
and our eyes meet
and I feel so comfortable

Sometimes I am
afraid to do something
and our eyes meet
and I feel so confident

Sometimes I
don't know if I have
made the right decision
and our eyes meet
and I feel so reassured

Sometimes I am
very confused
and our eyes meet
and I know I am understood

When our eyes meet
the love we have for each other
shines through
giving me such strength
*   and happiness*
When our eyes meet
our hearts unite
and your love
creates a protective rainbow over me
and the world becomes
*   a peaceful garden*

I Love You
Even More Today

I remember when we first met
I remember
the places we used to go together
the special things we used to talk about
the songs that were popular then
and the very first feeling of love
    that I had for you
These are touching memories
but what is even more beautiful
is that as the days pass
our love just seems to grow and grow
Our love is a continuation from the past
a monument to today
and the strength of our future
I love the memories we share
and I love sharing today with you

I can't say I love you enough
because it is the most
beautiful, complete feeling
I have ever had
Over and over again
I love you

Thank you for being in my dance
You are my dance
Thank you for being in my solace
You are my solace
Thank you for being in my fervor
You are my fervor
Thank you for being in my sun
You are my sun
Thank you for being in my life
You are my life

I Love You
More Than Words
Can Express

I may not always thank you
for loving me
or tell you how important
you are to me
I may not always express
how much you are a part of me
or how unhappy I would be
if you were not here
But I always feel these things

When two people are as close
as we are
words are not always necessary
But just so you know
how strongly I feel about you
I want to say to you now
that I love you
more than
words can
express

Nothing in My Life Is More Important Than Our Love

I always thought that
what I do each day
is so vital
what I say each day
is so necessary
what I learn each day
is so stimulating
but I have found out that
what I feel each day
is the most gratifying
and my love for you
is the deepest
feeling I have
Thank you for your love
It is the most important and
beautiful part of my life

Our Love Can Last Forever If We Both Want It To

I want to have
a lasting relationship with you
I know that this will mean that
we both must work hard
to please each other
to help each other
to be fair and honest with each other
to accept each other as we really are

Our love can last forever
if we want it to
We both must work hard
to keep our individuality
yet also become one with each other
to remain strong and supportive of each other
in adverse times as well as in good times
to be exciting and interesting
to ourselves and to each other

We both must work hard
to always consider each other
the most important person in the world
to always consider love
the most important emotion
that we can feel
to always consider our relationship
the most serious and significant
union of two people

Even though it may not always be easy
to have a lasting relationship
working hard is very easy
when the results can be
the beauty of a loving and lasting
us
I love you

You Are My World, You Are My Love

What if we had never met?
What would I be doing?
What kind of life would I have?
I often think about these things
and I always come to the same conclusion

Without you
I would be an extremely unhappy person
living an unhappy life
I know that we met for a reason
and that reason was that
you and I were meant to be
in love with each other

You and I were meant to be
a team giving us strength
to function happily in the world
I am so thankful that things
turned out the way they did
and we were brought together
You are my world
You are my love

I Promise That
I Will Love You

*I cannot promise you that
I will not change
I cannot promise you that
I will not have many different moods
I cannot promise you that
I will not hurt your feelings sometimes
I cannot promise you that
I will not be erratic
I cannot promise you that
I will always be strong
I cannot promise you that
my faults will not show*

But —
I do promise you that
I will always be supportive of you
I do promise you that
I will share all my thoughts
     and feelings with you
I do promise you that
I will give you freedom to be yourself
I do promise you that
I will understand everything that you do
I do promise you that
I will be completely honest with you
I do promise you that
I will laugh and cry with you
I do promise you that
I will help you achieve all your goals
But —
most of all
I do promise you that
I will love you

I Love You

When we first met
I held back so much
afraid to show
my deepest feelings

As I got to know you better
your gentleness and honesty
encouraged me to open up
and I started a trust
in you that I never had
with anyone else
Once I started to express
my feelings
I realized that
this is the only way
to have a relationship
It is such a
wonderful feeling
to let myself
be completely known to you
Thank you
so much
for showing me
what two people can
share together
I love you

About the Author

Susan Polis Schutz is an accomplished writer, poet, documentary filmmaker, and advocate for women's issues, the elderly, and dispelling the stigma of mental illness. She is a graduate of Rider University where she majored in English and biology and was later awarded an honorary doctor of laws degree. Together with her husband, Stephen Schutz, she cofounded Blue Mountain Arts, a popular publisher known for its distinctive greeting cards, gifts, and poetry books. Susan has been happily married to Stephen for forty-two years.

Susan is the author of many best-selling books of poetry illustrated by Stephen. Her first book, *Come Into the Mountains, Dear Friend*, was an instant success. It was followed by more titles, including *To My Daughter with Love on the Important Things in Life*, which has sold over 1.6 million copies and led *Time* magazine to proclaim her "the reigning star" in high emotion. Its companion volume, *To My Son with Love*, has also enjoyed a wide audience. Susan's poems and Stephen's artwork have been published on over 425 million greeting cards worldwide.

Following the tragic events of September 11, 2001, the Schutzes created a small book of Susan's poetry and Stephen's artwork entitled *One World, One Heart*. It was distributed free to over seven million people throughout the world with the hope that Susan's words would encourage people everywhere to put aside their differences and come together in peace, understanding, and love.

Susan's latest undertaking is creating documentary films that make a difference in people's lives with her production company, IronZeal Films. Her films have been shown on PBS stations throughout the country and include *Anyone and Everyone*, which features a diverse group of parents and their gay children discussing their experiences; *Following Dreams*, which tells the stories of people who have overcome all odds and misfortunes to pursue their life dreams; and *The Misunderstood Epidemic: Depression*, which seeks to bring greater attention to this debilitating illness and to help people and family members understand and empathize with individuals affected by depression. Her newest film, *Over 90 and Loving It*, will air in spring 2011.